Wings

LES ASSELSTINE

Steck-Vaughn.

HOUGHTON MIFFLIN HARCOURT

10801 N. Mopac Expressway
Building # 3
Austin, TX 78759
1.800.531.5015

Steck-Vaughn is a trademark of HMH Supplemental Publishers Inc.
registered in the United States of America and/or other jurisdictions.
All inquiries should be mailed to HMH Supplemental Publishers Inc.,
P.O. Box 27010, Austin, TX 78755.

Ru'bicon
www.rubiconpublishing.com

Project Editors: Miriam Bardswich, Kim Koh
Editor: Kermin Bhot
Editorial Assistant: Dawna McKinnon
Creative Director: Jennifer Drew
Art Director: Jen Harvey
Designer: Waseem Bashar
Cover image–U.S. Air Force photo by Staff Sgt. Tony R. Tolley;
title page–iStockphoto

Printed in Singapore

ISBN: 978-1-4190-2413-9
4 5 6 7 8 9 10 11 12 13 2016   22 21 20 19 18 17 16 15 14 13
A B C D E F G

CONTENTS

4 Introduction

6 Those Magnificent Men in Their Flying Machines
Up, down, flying around — hold onto your seat as you read these lyrics!

8 Flying Firsts
Airplanes have changed since they were invented in 1903.
Check out the highlights of airplane history in this article.

14 Who Killed the Red Baron?
Imagine being chased by Germany's ace fighter pilot — then watching him go down in a fiery crash. That's what happens in this incredible personal account.

18 Scare Mail
The first airmail pilots had deadly jobs, as this article reveals.

22 Acrobatics in the Sky
Air acrobatics have been turning heads and stomachs since the 1920s. Read this newspaper article about death-defying stunts.

26 Crashed — Twice!
A scenic flight through the mountains takes a terrifying turn in this graphic story.

30 King of Combat
Check out the parts that make the F-15 one of the most famous fighter planes in this illustration.

32 Interview with a Pilot
Pilot Melissa Chalmers shares her exciting experiences in this BOLDPRINT interview.

36 Calvin and Hobbes
What happens when Calvin takes command of a jet airliner?
Find out in this comic strip.

38 Fit to Fly a President
Air Force One provides a state-of-the-art office for the U.S. president as he travels. Read this article about an anything-but-ordinary airplane.

40 Roller Coaster in the Sky
NASA calls this plane the Weightless Wonder, but others call it the Vomit Comet! This article explains why.

42 Snowstorm
Two 12-year-olds take a flight and encounter a blinding blizzard.
Find out their fate in this frightening fiction excerpt.

8

14

42

I sweep the skies with fire and steel
My highway is the cloud
I swoop, I soar, aloft I wheel
My engine laughing loud ...

— Gordon Boshel

THOSE MAGNIFICENT IN THEIR FLYING

Lyrics by Ron Goodwin

Up, down, flying around

Looping the loop and defying the ground

They're all frightfully keen

Those Magnificent Men in their Flying Machines

They can fly upside down with their feet in the air

They don't think of danger they really don't care.

Newton would think he had made a mistake

To see those young men and the chances they take ...

defying: *challenging*
Newton: *Sir Isaac Newton was a scientist famous for discovering the laws of gravity*

MEN
MACHINES

wrap up

Create an image to illustrate the action in one of the verses of the song.

FLYING FIRSTS

warm up

Scan the pictures in this article. In a small group, share what you know about one of the aircraft or pilots.

Airplanes have come a long way since they were invented in 1903. From the 12-horsepower engine of the Wright brothers' first plane to the stealth bomber, there have been major changes. Here are a few of the most significant people, aircraft, and events in airplane history.

stealth: *design style that makes an aircraft difficult to see*

The First Airplane

Wilbur and Orville Wright

On December 17, 1903, Orville and Wilbur Wright completed the first successful airplane flight with their Wright Flyer. It only lasted for 12 seconds and covered a distance of 120 feet. The Flyer was a heavier-than-air craft powered by a 12-horsepower engine. It had three more successful flights before a gust of wind flipped it over. On the last flight, Wilbur flew the plane 852 feet in 59 seconds.

Wright Flyer

FYI

A Boeing 747 aircraft's wingspan is longer than the Wright brothers' first flight.

All Wright Brothers Images–U.S. Air Force Photo

The Spruce Goose

During World War II, troops and supplies were carried overseas on large ships. The ships were slow and often in danger of being shot by torpedoes fired from submarines. Henry Kaiser and Howard Hughes received a government contract to make a flying boat. The project took a long time and went over budget. Kaiser backed out, but Howard Hughes went on to invest his own money building this flying boat, which he called the *Spruce Goose*. The war was over before the plane was ready to fly. It never went into use, but Hughes actually flew it a little more than a mile just to prove that it could fly.

Nonstop Across the Atlantic

Imagine flying through clouds, heavy fog, rain, and snow while sitting in an open cockpit.

Add to that some engine problems and instruments that won't work because they are frozen or covered with ice. This describes the record-breaking flight of Captain John Alcock and Lieutenant Arthur Whitten Brown. They were the first fliers to make a nonstop flight across the Atlantic Ocean. They left Newfoundland on June 14, 1919 and, approximately 16 hours later, made a crash landing in an Irish marsh.

Vickers-Vimy Biplane

Charles Lindbergh

The *Spirit of St. Louis*

Charles Lindbergh was the first person to fly solo across the Atlantic Ocean. In 1927, he flew from Long Island, New York to Paris, France — traveling approximately 3,500 miles in 33 hours in his plane the *Spirit of St. Louis*. The plane was specially designed with the journey in mind. In order to keep the airplane light so that it could hold as much fuel as possible, it did not have a parachute, radio, gas gauge, or front window! During the flight, there were times when he flew only 10 feet above the waves of the ocean to avoid bad weather. He was awarded $25,000 for his accomplishment.

Amelia Earhart

Amelia Earhart was the first woman to complete a solo flight across the Atlantic Ocean. She left Newfoundland on May 20, 1932 and reached the coast of Ireland the next day — a 15-hour flight. In 1922, she broke the women's altitude record, flying up to 14,000 feet. Amelia Earhart disappeared in 1937 while flying over the Pacific Ocean. Although the U.S. government spent over $4 million searching for her, she was never found. To this day, no one knows what happened to Amelia Earhart.

The First Jet Airplane

The idea of a jet engine was first suggested by the famous scientist Sir Isaac Newton in the 17th century. He said that if an explosion was aimed in one direction, it would create a force in the opposite direction. In jet engines, air is taken in, pushed together by fans, and mixed with fuel. The mixture explodes. The force of the exhaust going out the back of the engine causes movement in the opposite direction — making the jet travel forward.

During the 1930s, two men worked separately on the development of the jet engine. Even though they never worked with each other, Frank Whittle and Hans Von Obain both came up with the same solution. Some people give them joint credit for creating the jet-powered airplane. However, the actual first flight was achieved when Von Obain and Ernst Heinkel built the Heinkel He178. They had their first successful flight on August 27, 1939.

Faster Than the Speed of Sound

Chuck Yeager began flying in World War II. After the war, he was assigned to test the Bell X-1 experimental plane and see if it could fly faster than the speed of sound. On October 14, 1947, he succeeded. Yeager renamed the plane the *Glamorous Glennis* in honor of his wife.

Jet Aircraft–Rue des Archives/Granger Collection, New York; Chuck Yeager-U.S. Air Force Photo; Bell X1-U.S. Air Force Photo

Higher Than Ever Before

When it comes to flying high, the most successful solution has been to use the energy source that is most obvious — the sun. The Helios Prototype operates from energy collected from the sun.

On August 13, 2001, NASA staff waited for the clouds over Hawaii to clear prior to starting the historic flight that set the altitude record for a non-rocket-powered aircraft. The flight was operated by several different pilots with remote controls.

There was no one in the aircraft. The pilots were guided by images from a camera mounted on Helios. They guided the craft to a record height of over 96,500 feet. This is more than three times higher than the flight of a commercial aircraft.

CHECKPOINT

Why do you think they waited for the clouds to go away?

Helios Prototype

Helios–U.S. Air Force Photo

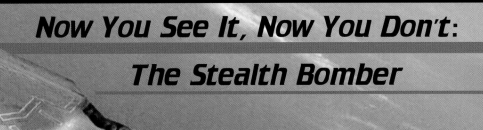

Now You See It, Now You Don't: The Stealth Bomber

The stealth bomber was designed to fly long distances and carry large weapons. Most importantly, it was designed to be as invisible as possible.

The stealth bomber's dark colors make it invisible at night, and its shape makes it difficult for observers to know which way it is going. The unique shape of the plane means that its engines don't need to work as hard as the engines of other planes. This means less noise and less heat. In addition, the engines are inside the plane so that the sound is muffled and the exhaust is cooled before it gets out, which makes it less visible in the air.

The shape of the plane and the materials used on its exterior make it difficult to be picked up by radar. The radar's radio beams are either absorbed or scattered when they hit the stealth.

All of these design features mean that the only time you are likely to see the stealth bomber is when it is parked on the runway.

wrap up

1. Write a newspaper headline for each of the Flying Firsts.

2. Find out more about one of these Flying Firsts in your school library. Write a one-minute radio news spot reporting what you learned.

unique: *one of a kind*
radar: *a device that uses radio waves to detect objects*

Stealth Bomber-U.S. Air Force Photo

WHO KILLED THE
RED BARON?

warm up

Think of movies or TV shows that you have seen about combat pilots. What are some of the moves they used to escape enemy fire?

*I*t was April 21, 1918. Lieutenant Wilfred R. May, a Canadian pilot with Britain's Royal Air Force, was being chased by German ace Baron Manfred Von Richthofen. The German pilot was also known as the Red Baron because of the color of his triplane. May's guns had jammed in battle, and he couldn't return fire. Pursued by Richthofen, May headed for the British lines.

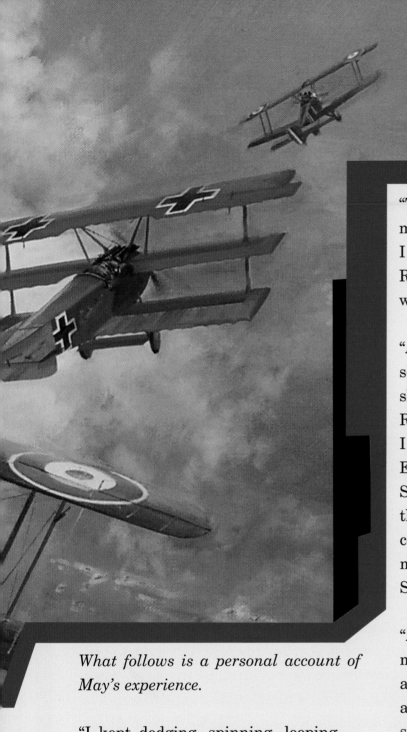

"The only thing that saved me was my awful flying! I didn't know what I was doing myself, and I'm certain Richthofen couldn't figure out what I was going to do next.

"After almost slicing off the tops of some of those hedges I found myself skimming the surface of the Somme River. ... I knew I was a sitting duck. I must have died a thousand deaths. Every second I expected the stream of Spandau bullets to tear a hole right through me. ... In my mind's eye, I could see the leather-helmeted head of my enemy, his goggled eyes lining his Spandau for the kill.

"Another plane flitted past the tail of my eye, followed by a burst of gunfire and — a sudden silence. As I threw a fearful glance over my shoulder, I saw Richthofen do a half-spin and hit the ground. A second glance showed me that the second plane was one of our own."

May's rescuer was the leader of his squadron, Captain Roy Brown — a friend since school days.

What follows is a personal account of May's experience.

"I kept dodging, spinning, looping — doing every trick I knew — until I ran out of sky and was forced to hedge-hop over the ground. Richthofen was giving me burst after burst from his twin Spandau machine guns.

CHECKPOINT
Visualize the scenes as you read.

Spandau: *German-made*

Manfred Von Richthofen

Brown's combat report states:

"At 10:35 AM I observed two Albatrosses burst into flames and crash. Dived on a large formation of 15 to 20 Albatross scouts, D.5s, and Fokker triplanes, two of which got on my tail, and I came out. Went back again and dived on a pure red triplane which was firing on Lieutenant (Wilfred) May. I got a long burst into him, and he went down vertical and was observed to crash by Lieutenant (Francis) Mellersh and Lieutenant May. I fired on two more but did not get them."

Though Britain's Royal Air Force gave official credit to Roy Brown for Richthofen's death, there are many people who believe differently. For example, Australia has always *claimed that it was their fire from the ground that brought down the Red Baron.*

The debate over the events of that day is still alive. Forensic experts feel that the angle of the shot that killed the Red Baron doesn't fit with the location of Brown's airplane. Even though Brown fired at the plane, his bullets were not likely responsible for the kill. At the same time, the Australians and others were also trying to shoot down the Baron's plane. Many people continue to ask the question, "Who really killed the Red Baron?"

Albatrosses, D.5s, Fokker triplanes:
fighter planes

CHECKPOINT
Note that an ace would not be credited with downing an enemy plane unless there was confirmation.

Manfred Von Richthofen (1892-1918)—Granger Collection, New York; all other images—iStockphoto

New Technology

Airplanes were still very new at the beginning of World War I — and very fragile. At first, planes were only used for checking enemy positions and didn't even have weapons. Flying was dangerous enough. But it wasn't long before pilots were carrying guns and dogfights became part of the war in the air.

As WWI continued, scientists and engineers in Germany, France, and England worked hard to gain an advantage. Planes became more powerful and more maneuverable. Steel plates were added for protection and guns were mounted onto the planes or built in. One challenge for pilots was to fire a gun without shooting their own propellers. This problem was solved on one British plane by mounting the propeller behind the pilot. Other planes were modified so that the gun and propeller were synchronized — timed in such a way that the bullets passed between the moving propeller blades.

maneuverable: *able to change position*

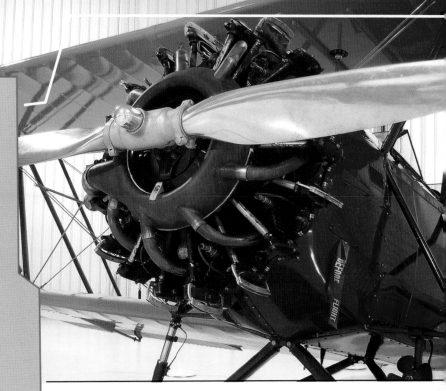

wrap up

1. In a group of three, role-play a discussion between Roy Brown, Wilfred May, and an Australian artillery soldier about their encounters with the Red Baron's plane.

2. Research information about a modern fighter plane and compare it to one of the planes from World War I. In what ways is the new plane very different from the old one? Present your information in a chart.

WEB CONNECTIONS

Use the Internet to find information about the Red Baron. Who do you think killed him? Share your opinion with a partner and defend your choice.

SCARE MAIL

How would the world be different if there was no airmail, and the only way to deliver letters was by boat, train, or truck?

CHECKPOINT

As you read this article, think about the claim made by postal-delivery people that nothing can stop the mail.

Just 30 minutes into his first flight as a U.S. Air Mail pilot, Dean Smith discovered that his new job could be deadly. Without warning, the engine of his de Havilland DH-4 airplane suddenly quit. Below lay mile after mile of forest and a tiny clearing that was the only hope for a safe landing.

Fighting rain and a steady wind, Smith steered his tiny, powerless aircraft toward the clearing. The plane narrowly cleared the bank of trees and swooped to the ground. But just as Smith's landing gear touched the earth, it slammed into a hidden ledge, crumpling the DH-4 like a piece of paper. The crash ejected Smith,

narrowly: *barely*

who plowed into the brush with his seat belt still across his lap.

A local farmer used his horse and wagon to carry Smith and his mail bags to the nearest railroad station. There, the bruised and battered pilot continued his journey by train. He had survived his first crash but it would not be his last. In the early days of airmail, pilots risked their lives on every flight. ...

FYI

The U.S. Air Mail Service began May 15, 1918. Second Assistant Postmaster General Otto Praeger believed planes could deliver mail faster than trains.

The first Air Mail route ran Washington, D.C. to New York City. For a skilled pilot, this route was relatively easy. It featured prominent landmarks and fields for emergency landings. But when the postal service decided to extend Air Mail across Pennsylvania's Allegheny Mountains to Cleveland, danger arose.

The Alleghenies were heavily forested, without many navigation landmarks. They often lay hidden in clouds, and were home to some of the worst weather in the East. ...

prominent: *important, famous*

If anyone could meet the challenge, the daring young pilots of the Air Mail service could. Many had flown in combat during World War I. Some had performed in barnstorming air shows. And as Air Mail expanded westward to Chicago and beyond, these men proved their bravery and resourcefulness again and again.

Pilot Frank Yeager even discovered a new way to fly in heavy fog. He drove his plane on the ground across 35 miles of foggy prairie, rising into the air only to hop the barbed-wire fences that stood in his way. …

Still, these early pilots faced deadly odds. Between October 1919 and July 1921, 26 Air Mail employees died in plane crashes — more than one fatality per month. The average Air Mail pilot could expect to fly less than two years before dying on the job.

barnstorming: *doing sightseeing flights and stunt flying at stops across the country*
resourcefulness: *ability to cope with difficult situations*

Thanks to the work of pilots, mechanics, engineers, and administrators, airmail became steadily safer. Starting in 1920, pilots were issued parachutes. At first, many complained about having to carry them. But once a few lives were saved, they stopped complaining. New flight instruments and devices such as headlights on the wings made it easier for pilots to control and land their planes. And the quality of maintenance improved.

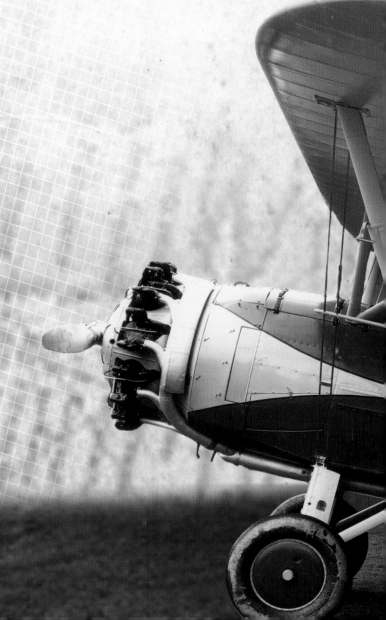

After a dramatic coast-to-coast flight in February 1921 proved mail could be flown at night, the U.S. government set up a system of light beacons and lighted airfields across the country. The beacons guided night fliers, and the lighted fields provided safe landing spots. ...

The safety record had already begun to improve, and it continued to do so. Between July of 1921 and September of 1922, not a single Air Mail employee died in a plane crash. By the end of 1923, pilot safety became a top priority of the Air Mail Service. And soon, as the small planes gave way to larger, more reliable ones, airmail became even safer.

---

beacons: *guiding or warning signals*

The first years of airmail had been dramatic and dangerous. One of the pilots who survived was Dean Smith, whose telegram to Air Mail headquarters after a crash in Iowa serves as one of the best reminders of the wild and woolly days of early airmail. It read simply:

"On Trip 4 westbound. Flying low. Engine quit. Only place to land on cow. Killed cow. Wrecked plane. Scared me. Smith."

wrap up

1. Write a help-wanted ad for a pilot to deliver airmail during the early 1920s. Include the qualities you would expect the pilot to have.

2. Over the years, airplanes have been used for many other important tasks. Research the roles airplanes have played in completing land surveys, searching for oil, fighting forest fires, serving isolated communities, advertising, or performing rescues. Prepare a short oral report for your group.

Acrobatics in the Sky

Air Acrobatics–Granger Collection, New York

warm up

With a partner, discuss the qualities that might make a person well suited for flying in an air show.

The air acrobatics craze of the 1920s was started by young pilots who had learned their skills dodging enemies during World War I. They were known as barnstormers. They flew to a rural area, found a farmer's field, buzzed a nearby town, dropped advertising leaflets, and then drew the crowd to the field.

Pilots took people for rides for $1.00 each and put on spectacular shows. They flew upside down, chased each other's tails, and thrilled audiences with circles, loops, and spins. They showed off by wing walking and flying through barns.

The tricks were exciting but often very risky. By 1927, air safety regulations were passed, but the shows remained popular.

The following article describes a modern-day air show featuring a vintage airplane.

Pilot turns heads, stomachs at air show

Chris Hubbuch, *Winona Daily News*,
July 4, 2005

The smoke was on. The speed was up.

A little before 11 AM Sunday morning, Bill Blank zoomed low over the airstrip at Winona's Max Conrad Field at about 160 mph, white smoke trailing from his small red plane.

He flipped the plane over, then aimed it straight up at a low ceiling of gray clouds, where it seemed to hang motionless before it crested the loop and plunged back toward the earth.

"There goes my stomach," said one observer with two feet on the ground.

---

crested: *reached the top of*

Blank, a 62-year-old amateur pilot from La Crosse, Wisconsin, put on an aerobatic show of loops, rolls, and spins for about 150 people at the 22nd annual Breakfast and Air Show.

The flight plan — a series of parabolas and other squiggles that could have passed for someone's calculus homework — hung from a metal clip on the dash of the two-seat Super Decathlon airplane.

CHECKPOINT

Notice how pilots make ground crew aware of their plans.

"In case I forget," Blank said.

The retired ophthalmologist started flying in 1968, but didn't get into aerobatics until he took a class in 1977, after a veteran pilot from WWII said it would make him a better pilot.

Since then he has gone on to perform in more than a hundred air shows. He has also taught more than 1,200 hours of acrobatic flying to other pilots.

The most difficult maneuver, Blank says, is the outside roll, in which he flies the plane through a loop upside-down, with a force about three times as strong as gravity pulling him up out of his seat.

"You feel like you are going to get shot out of the plane," he said.

---

parabolas: *bowl-shaped patterns*
calculus: *branch of higher mathematics*
ophthalmologist: *eye doctor*

Lincoln Beachey

Risky Business

Although air shows are very exciting to watch, they can be extremely dangerous. Over the years, the technology of airplanes has improved and accidents are less likely to happen. However the speed of planes has also increased and whenever pilots perform in an air show, they are taking a risk. Lincoln Beachey was one of the first stunt pilots and was considered by many to be the most skilled. He was best known for his amazing loops and dives. While performing for an audience during the Panama-Pacific International Exposition in San Francisco, the wings came off Beachey's plane, causing it to crash into the ground at top speed. He was killed instantly.

Accidents, however, do not always end tragically. On August 24, 2005, a jet from the Snowbirds aerobatics team was traveling to Thunder Bay, Ontario, Canada to perform at a show when the jet's engine failed, causing it to crash into a rural field. The pilot, Andy Mackay, was able to safely exit the plane and parachuted down into the woods below, where he was rescued by a man who saw the crash.

LINCOLN BEACHEY–Granger Collection, New York

The Thunderbirds Aerial Demonstration Team

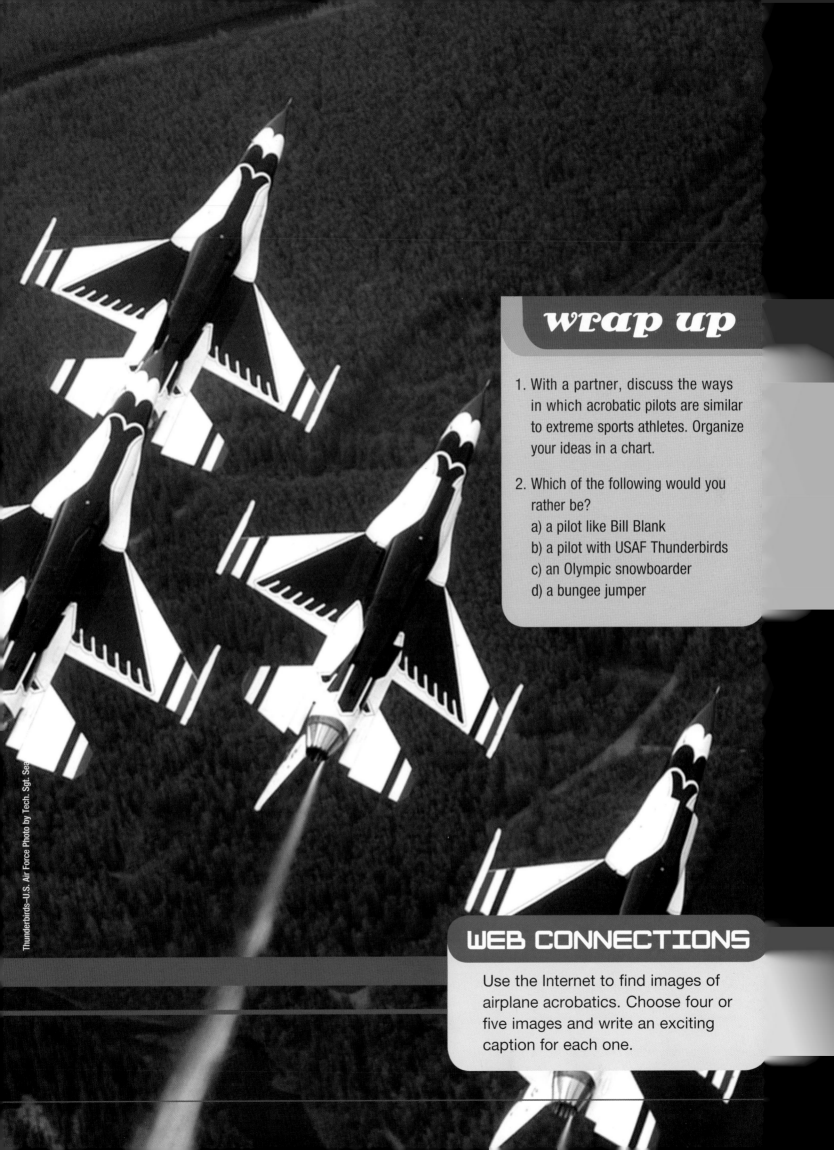

wrap up

1. With a partner, discuss the ways in which acrobatic pilots are similar to extreme sports athletes. Organize your ideas in a chart.

2. Which of the following would you rather be?
   a) a pilot like Bill Blank
   b) a pilot with USAF Thunderbirds
   c) an Olympic snowboarder
   d) a bungee jumper

WEB CONNECTIONS

Use the Internet to find images of airplane acrobatics. Choose four or five images and write an exciting caption for each one.

CRASHED — TWICE!

ON A PALE JANUARY MORNING IN 2002, JUSTIN KIRKBRIDE TAKES HIS FRIENDS LARRY DIMOND AND TOMMY ROBBINS ON A SHORT SIGHTSEEING TOUR OF THE ROCKY MOUNTAINS IN COLORADO.

IT'S ALMOST TIME TO TURN BACK. I JUST WANT TO SHOW YOU ONE MORE CANYON.

JUSTIN, THIS HAS BEEN REALLY THRILLING. I CAN'T BELIEVE HOW CLEAR THE SKY IS.

HANG ON! I'M NOT SURE WHAT JUST HAPPENED BUT WE'RE DROPPING QUICKLY.

SEE IF YOU CAN LAND IT WHILE YOU STILL HAVE POWER!

I'M GOING TO TRY TO LAND IN THAT CLEARING. HANG ON!

SUDDENLY, THE WARNING BUZZER SOUNDS ...

PUTT PUTT PUTT·T·T·T

THERE GOES MY COMMERCIAL FLYING CAREER.

Illustrated by DAVID PIETILA

I DON'T KNOW IF I GOT THROUGH. I NEED TO GET TO HIGHER GROUND TO TRY MY CELL PHONE.

AFTER HOURS OF WALKING THROUGH KNEE-DEEP SNOW ...

HEY! OVER HERE!

THEY AREN'T TURNING. THEY MUST NOT HAVE SEEN ME. I HAVE TO KEEP GOING. IF I STOP NOW WE WILL ALL FREEZE TO DEATH.

TWO HOURS LATER JUSTIN TRIES THE PHONE AGAIN.

HELLO ... HELLO? THIS IS JUSTIN KIRKBRIDE, MY PLANE CRASHED AND ...

HIS CALL GOES THROUGH!

20 MINUTES LATER ...

I'LL BE FINE. YOU NEED TO FIND LARRY AND TOMMY.

WE'LL HAVE YOU AT THE HOSPITAL IN JUST A FEW MINUTES.

DURANGO CIVIL AIR PATROL PUTS JUSTIN ON A HELICOPTER.

3:15 AM — JUSTIN DECIDES TO JOIN THE RESCUE TO HELP LOCATE THE PLANE.

WE NEED TO MARK THE LOCATION. I'M JUST GOING TO CIRCLE ONCE MORE.

THERE IT IS! I SEE THE LIGHT REFLECTING ON THE PLANE!

AFTER HOURS OF SEARCHING, RESCUE WORKERS HAVE FOUND NO SIGN OF TOMMY OR LARRY.

WE'VE ASKED FOR HELP FROM KIRTLAND AIR FORCE BASE. THEY'RE SENDING TWO CHOPPERS.

wrap up

1. List instances where Justin demonstrated leadership.

2. With a partner, discuss how Justin may have felt when he had to leave his friends behind.

KING OF COMBAT

Shortly after airplanes were invented they were used in combat. The F-15 was created in the early 1970s and is one of the most famous fighter planes. The F-15 flies in all different kinds of weather and is known for its ability to move very quickly in different directions. It also has amazing electronic equipment and firepower. Check out what makes it move!

flap: moves downward during takeoff and landing to increase the amount of force from the wing

wing spars: titanium support structure inside the wing

titanium: *a strong metal*

cockpit: seats the pilot and allows him or her to see 360° around the aircraft

air brake: lifts up to quickly slow the aircraft down

F-15E Strike Eagle–Graphic by Virginia Reyes, AFNEWS/NSPD

radar warning receiver: detects radio emissions of radar systems from the ground or another aircraft

vertical stabilizer and horizontal stabilizer: help to balance and steer the aircraft

engine: provides power for the flight and pushes the aircraft forward

wrap up

Choose one part of the F-15. Write a paragraph describing what would happen if the part was damaged while the plane was in the air.

INTERVIEW WITH A PILOT

warm up

Imagine you are flying a large airliner. What do you think it would feel like?

BOLDPRINT interviews Melissa Chalmers, a pilot flying for Air Canada. At the time of the interview, Chalmers was a first officer on an Airbus A320.

BOLDPRINT: When did you first decide that you wanted to be a pilot?

Melissa Chalmers: When I was four or five years old, my mother took a floatplane trip around a lake and brought me along. I thought it was such an exhilarating experience. I thought a lot about flying since then.

exhilarating: *exciting*

BP: How long did it take to get your wings?

MC: It took about six months to get my private license. It can be done much quicker. I later attended Sault College for flying and it was a two-year program that ran through the summers.

BP: What was the most difficult part of your flight training?

MC: Apart from having to deal with the ex-military flying instructors, the most difficult part was the instrument flight rating. It requires some mental gymnastics, but you get used to it pretty quickly. I wasn't great with visualizing directions in my head, but I soon caught on and now it's just natural for me.

BP: What was the first plane you flew on your own?

MC: I flew a Cessna 152 on my first flight. It's a small two-seater with a high wing, meaning the wings are at the top of the aircraft.

BP: Which school subjects would you recommend for students interested in becoming pilots?

MC: Take math, just so you're used to doing math in your head. Physics wouldn't hurt. I didn't take chemistry myself, but really wish I had. Business courses might help.

BP: What is the scariest experience you've had as a pilot?

MC: That's easy. Once when I was just transferred onto an airplane in Newfoundland, my captain wanted to show me how the autopilot worked. We used the autopilot down to 300 ft. It was very foggy out and it disconnected and the airplane dove down by itself. All

autopilot: *device for keeping an aircraft on a set course*

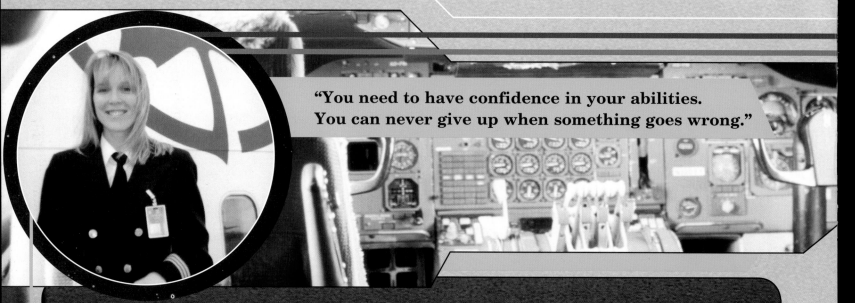

I could see were spruce trees pointing up through the foggy mist and we both pulled back on the controls so as not to hit them. Then the captain tried to land the aircraft, almost hitting the wing on the ground. We made it on the runway safely and were both very relieved to be alive.

CHECKPOINT

How do you think you would feel if you were put in this situation?

BP: How many years have you been flying?

MC: I started flying in 1987, so I guess that makes it 19 years.

BP: What is the most exciting thing about being a pilot?

MC: The most exciting thing for me is just flying the airplane. As an airline pilot, I have lots of fun flying new airplanes and meeting new people. The best thing is the layovers in interesting places around the world. You see so many things that most people don't get to see. You use your mind, talk to other people, travel, and play the best video game of your life.

layovers: *short stays between flights*

Photo Courtesy of Melissa Chalmers; Cockpit–iStockphoto; Airplane–indexopen

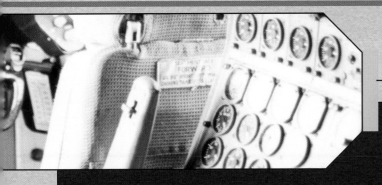

BP: What is required to be a good pilot?

MC: You need to have confidence in your abilities. You can never give up when something goes wrong. You need to be able to listen to others and also to think first before acting. Social ability is an asset, although I think that is something I acquired because of my job.

CHECKPOINT
What do you think social ability is?

You need to be able to entertain yourself and you need to be able to speak up when things aren't going the way they should. You have to be assertive.

BP: What are the greatest benefits of being a pilot?

MC: The hours are eventually very flexible. There is a lot of job satisfaction. You get to travel, which can be really fun. You get to have many friends all over the place. Once you are a captain, you get to run the operation the way you like things to be.

assertive: *continually confident*
flexible: *changed easily*

BP: So once you're done your training, what do you do then?

MC: There are many job options for pilots. You could get a job with a company flying their corporate jets. There are jobs with the government helping put out fires. You can instruct people to fly. That would be a good job for someone who doesn't want to move around or spend a lot of time away with an airline job. There is also traffic reporting, tourist rides, and banner towing. And of course you could always have a career in the military.

FYI

Most model airplane clubs have special Learn to Fly programs. These programs teach about the controls of the aircraft and other important skills needed to fly an airplane.

wrap up

1. With a partner, discuss what Melissa Chalmers enjoys about being a pilot. What appeals to you the most? The least?

2. Design a help-wanted ad for an airline pilot. Be sure to include qualities that the airline is looking for and the benefits of the job.

CALVIN PILOTS THE JET AIRLINER ACROSS THE COUNTRY AT 35,000 FEET.

4-5

HE IS GIVEN CLEARANCE TO LAND. BUT WHAT'S THIS? A PLANE FROM A RIVAL AIRLINE IS MAKING FOR THE SAME RUNWAY TO SHAVE PRECIOUS MINUTES OFF ITS SCHEDULE!

WATTERSON

THE OTHER PILOT TRIES TO CUT CALVIN OFF WITH A SUDDEN DROP IN ALTITUDE!

CALVIN SWITCHES ON THE "FASTEN SEAT BELT" LIGHT IN THE CABIN, AND DOES A BARREL ROLL!

AT 5 Gs, CALVIN HOPES NOT TO BLACK OUT!

wrap up

In this comic strip, Calvin used his imagination to dream up an unbelievable story. Use your imagination to create a short episode about yourself and an airplane.

FIT TO FLY A PRESIDENT

Air Force One—U.S. Air Force Photo

warm up

Have you ever been on an airplane? If so, what did you like most and least about it?

Air Force One is the name given to whatever plane is carrying the president of the United States. Usually that plane is one of two almost identical 747s that have been customized for the president. From the outside, they look very similar to the 747 jetliners that are used to carry passengers on regular flights. However, the inside tells a different story.

customized: *changed to suit a specific customer*

The airplane provides a state-of-the-art home and office for the president while in the air. There are also private washroom facilities, a workout room, and two galleys for meal preparation. The plane carries more than 50,000 gallons of fuel and enough food for more than 2,000 meals! It can also be refueled while flying.

CHECKPOINT

Why do you think this is important?

Having a medical room and a pharmacy on the plane means that the doctor who flies with the president is well equipped to provide emergency care. These features allow the president to stay in the air for

state-of-the-art: *highly developed*
galleys: *kitchens on a ship or airplane*

a long time, which is important in an emergency situation.

Air Force One offers the latest in communication technology, with more than 200 miles of wiring. There are phones, faxes, and computer connections so that the president can contact people around the world. It also has technology to provide protection if it is under attack — but information about this is top secret!

Fantasy Flights

You don't have to be a president to fly in luxury! Some airlines are now offering perks ranging from world-class chefs to luxury beds. Passengers can order their own meals from a gourmet cuisine selection prepared by international chefs. When it's time for a nap, first class seats transform to a bed with the finest linens and a down-filled duvet. Sleepy passengers can relax in luxury in a designer pyjama suit, soft eyeshades, and warm terrycloth socks. Remember to search for the perks on your next flight!

FYI

Every Air Force One flight is considered a military operation. Special crews carefully inspect the plane and runway before each flight.

wrap up

Imagine you are a passenger on Air Force One. Write an email to a friend describing your flight.

Roller Coaster in the Sky

warm up

Think about a time when you or one of your friends had motion sickness. When did it happen? What do you think was the cause?

Many people experience motion sickness when they are riding in something that makes sudden or unexpected movements — airplanes during turbulent weather, ships during storms, or amusement park rides. A person with motion sickness often feels dizzy and sick to his or her stomach. This is because the inner ear

turbulent: *violent*

is telling the brain that the person's balance is being affected by movement, although the body is still.

The Vomit Comet is one plane that has many of its passengers reaching for their throw-up bags. NASA refers to the KC-135A as the Weightless Wonder, but rookies who have experienced the ride nicknamed it the Vomit Comet.

NASA uses the modified KC-135A airplane for training astronauts. Compared to regular airplanes, it has additional power so that it can climb quickly and handle the pressure of sudden changes in direction. During each training flight, the Comet quickly climbs to 32,000 ft. and

modified: *slightly changed*

Aboard the NASA KC-135A airplane

If you are prone to motion sickness, there are medications that you can take. You can also try to prevent motion sickness by relaxing before a trip, riding in a part of the vehicle where sudden motion might be less, or by making sure you can look ahead to see the motion that your inner ear is feeling.

prone: *likely to be or act a certain way*

FYI

Your inner ear contains very small particles that are called otoliths or ear stones. When your head moves, these otoliths move and touch sensory cells that then tell your brain whether or not you are balanced. If the message from your inner ear is different from the message from your eyes, your brain may become confused causing you to feel dizzy or even sick to your stomach.

then goes through a series of 30 to 40 climbs and dives. During each climb passengers feel almost twice as heavy as normal and during each dive they feel weightless for 20 to 25 seconds. The dives are intended to simulate weightlessness.

CHECKPOINT

This is called microgravity. The passengers feel weightless because they are falling at the same speed as the dive of the airplane.

Pilots of the Comet say that about one-third of their passengers become violently ill, the next third moderately ill, and the final third not at all.

simulate: *imitate*

wrap up

Design a poster advertising rides in the Vomit Comet.

WEB CONNECTIONS

Use the Internet to find two facts about the Vomit Comet not mentioned in this article. In a small group, share the information you find.

SNOWSTORM

BY DAVID BOYD

Excerpt from *Earthwatch*

warm up

What is the most frightening thing that has ever happened to you? Share your story with another classmate.

The weather had changed quickly overnight as a cold wave surged down from the Arctic. But Wordsy and Jess, bundled up in thick wool sweaters and with their ski jackets on the seats beside them, were not worried about the cold as they waited inside Mr. Lalonde's plane. …

surged: *increased suddenly*

Soon the plane was racing down the runway. … Jess turned and grinned at Wordsy. They had both flown in big commercial airplanes before, but flying in a small plane was a new adventure. Somehow it seemed more exciting for just the three of them to be in a small plane, than to be sitting with hundreds of other people in a big jet.

CHECKPOINT
How do you feel about this statement?

Jess peered out her window eagerly to see if she could spot Porcupine Mountain. She was studying the landscape so hard that it took her a couple of minutes to realize that large snowflakes were floating by her window. ... The flakes were coming down fast and Mr. Lalonde turned on the wipers as the snow began to obscure the windshield.

Wordsy's face was pressed against the window as well, as he watched the giant snowflakes swirl past. It seemed as if they appeared out of nowhere, and he noticed how some of them clung to the wing of the plane for a few moments, only to be swept away again by the force of the wind. He looked up as he heard Mr. Lalonde contact the air traffic controller in Timmins.

"Timmins," said Mr. Lalonde tersely, "can I have a weather update, please?"

Wordsy watched Mr. Lalonde speaking into his small microphone, but he couldn't hear the controller's reply without headphones so he turned back to the window. He was surprised to see that the snow was descending even faster now, and the view through the window was becoming blurred by flakes that quickly turned to slush.

---

obscure: *hide from view*

tersely: *short, tensely*

Jess was listening to the radio transmission and she heard the controller advise that the skies were clear over Timmins, but that sudden squalls were now being reported in their area.

CHECKPOINT

What problems could this cause for the plane?

"No kidding," said Mr. Lalonde to the controller. "The flakes are as large as footballs up here. Visibility is becoming a problem."

"Advise you descend 2,000 feet," said the raspy voice of the controller.

---

squalls: *violent winds*
raspy: *harsh*

"Roger," replied Mr. Lalonde, and the plane gradually lost height.

FYI

Roger is a word used in radio and signaling to say that a message has been received and understood.

Jess pulled off her headphones and turned to look at Wordsy in the rear seat. He was still staring out his window, almost mesmerized by the patterns of thick flakes. The light within the cabin had faded as the storm increased, so Mr. Lalonde reached above himself to snap on a light. As he did,

---

mesmerized: *stared as if hypnotized*

Wordsy pulled himself away from the window again and saw Jess watching him. He immediately caught the look of worry on her face and he tried to smile reassuringly. Planes must get caught in snowstorms all the time, he thought.

Suddenly, a sharp bang resounded through the cabin. Smoke began pouring from the plane's engine, and a spray of caramel-colored oil hit the windshield. The wipers began to slap the oil back and forth, quickly making it impossible to see outside.

CHECKPOINT

As you read, imagine how Mr. Lalonde, Jess, and Wordsy feel.

"What the…," exclaimed Mr. Lalonde and he quickly raised the controller again.

"Timmins, we've got trouble here!" He scanned his instrument panel as he spoke: the oil gauge was giving a crazy reading. Then, there was the most deadly sound of all — silence! — as the plane's propeller stopped and the whine of the engine died.

"Engine out, Timmins! Repeat! Engine out!" yelled Mr. Lalonde. He turned to the children and saw the color drain from their faces. "Put your seat belts on, kids!" he ordered. Then he pulled open the small window on his left to help clear the smoke which was rapidly filling the cabin.

"Give us your position. Over," squawked the radio.

"Southeast edge of Night Hawk, as near as I can figure. Porcupine Mountain must be on my left, Timmins! We've got a real

visibility problem here. I'm losing altitude quickly, and I'm going to try and set it down on the water."

"Rescue services are being alerted. Stay on the air."

Jess was already wearing her seat belt and she sat nervously, her eyes transfixed by the smear of oil and slush on the windshield as the wipers swept back and forth. She forced herself to look away, and then realized that she was gripping the headset in her hands so tightly that she had begun to lose feeling in her fingers. Releasing the headset, she turned to look at Wordsy, fighting the feeling of panic rising within her.

Wordsy was fumbling frantically with his seatbelt and, when he finally managed to click the two ends together, he looked around the cabin nervously. The silence in the cabin was eerie and he struggled to find his voice. "Wh…what…happened?" he managed. Mr. Lalonde, concentrating solely on the plane, didn't seem to hear him and Wordsy became even more frightened.

Wordsy sat still, too scared to think, everything a blur of fear. He stared straight ahead, seeing nothing, barely aware now of what was happening. Jess tried to look through her window again, but the storm had become so intense now that she could only see her reflection in the glass. When she realized this she turned away quickly, for the girl looking back at her wore an expression of cold fear.

CHECKPOINT
Visualize the crash landing.

transfixed: *made motionless*

Paul Lalonde was using all the skills he possessed to force the plane onto the waters of Night Hawk Lake. As they descended, however, it became almost impossible to control the plane. The sudden loss of oil pressure had effectively seized the engine, and he knew that they were in very serious trouble.

"Lean forward with your head on your knees and your hands wrapped around your heads," Mr. Lalonde commanded Wordsy and Jess.

The impact, when it came, seemed to surprise Mr. Lalonde. The children heard him say, "I thought we were higher than…," and then the sounds of tearing fabric and the screech of metal upon metal drowned everything. The violence of the crash stunned Wordsy and the screams he heard were far away as if in a dream. …

seized: *stopped*

FYI

In the case of an airplane crash, the Federal Aviation Administration suggests crossing your hands on the seat in front of you and putting your head against your hands until the aircraft crashes. This position will reduce the impact to your head when the crash occurs.

wrap up

1. Imagine you are Jess or Wordsy. Write a diary or journal entry describing your thoughts and fears as the plane is about to crash.

2. Write an ending for the story in one or two paragraphs. Exchange your work with a partner.

ACKNOWLEDGMENTS

The publisher gratefully acknowledges the following for permission to reprint copyrighted material in this book.

Every reasonable effort has been made to trace the owners of copyrighted material and to make due acknowledgment. Any errors or omissions drawn to our attention will be gladly rectified in future editions.

Ron Goodwin: "Those Magnificent Men in Their Flying Machines." Words and Music by Ron Goodwin. © 1965 (renewed) EMI MILLER CATALOG INC. All Rights administered by EMI MILLER CATALOG INC. (Publishing) and ALFRED PUBLISHING CO., INC. (Print). All Rights Reserved.

Chris Hubbuch: "Pilot Turns Heads, Stomachs at Air Show." Permission courtesy of Winona Daily News © 2005.

CALVIN AND HOBBES © 1988 Watterson. Reprinted with permission of UNIVERSAL PRESS SYNDICATE. All rights reserved.

"Scare Mail" from WGBH Educational Foundation. Copyright © 2004 WGBH/Boston.

"Snowstorm" excerpted from *Earthwatch* by David Boyd. Copyright © 1990 Rubicon Publishing Inc.